CHAKRAS

A Comprehensive Guide To Comprehending Chakra Equilibrium For Facilitating Spiritual Enlightenment And Heightened Awareness

(Mindful Meditation For Enhancing Spiritual Well-being And Deepening Spiritual Development)

Norman Jenkinson

TABLE OF CONTENT

Healing The Root Chakra 1

Healing The Third Chakra 12

Techniques For Achieving Equilibrium In The Sacral Chakra..21

The Obstruction Or Hindrance Of The Sacral Chakra 26

Root Chakra Meditations 46

What Are Chakras? A Detailed Understanding.........65

Auras, How To See Them..76

The Importance Of Restoring And Harmonizing The Chakras..79

Equilibrium, Disequilibrium, And Obstructed Chakras..98

The Seven Chakras 123

Establishing A Connection With Your Chakras And Cultivating Self-Awareness..141

Preparing For Meditation..156

Healing The Root Chakra

The root chakra, known as 'muladhara' in Sanskrit, corresponds to the initial chakra within the 7 primary chakras. Each chakra is accompanied by a distinct symbol and color. The hue of a chakra is contingent upon the manner in which light is bent within your physique, as well as the frequency it encompasses. White light consists of a spectrum of seven colors. Upon entering the body, it undergoes refraction, giving rise to the manifestation of these seven colors. Subsequently, each of the seven chakras absorbs a specific portion of this light, corresponding to a distinct color. The color associated with the root chakra is crimson, and its symbol is depicted herein.

Within this chapter, let us delve further into the intrinsic nature of the root chakra and ascertain the methods through which its restoration may be achieved.

What are the Functions and Purposes of the Root Chakra?

The sacral energy center is situated at the anatomical base of your vertebral column and is regarded as the fundamental cornerstone of your overall being, specifically pertaining to your physicality. Its primary function is to furnish assistance and stability to your physique and psyche, thereby guaranteeing seamless interconnection between all the subsystems within your corporeal being. Additionally, it assumes the responsibility of ensuring your sense of security and safety. In addition, it is interconnected with the spinal cord, the musculature of the pelvic floor, and the initial three vertebrae, thereby encompassing any potential concerns associated with these regions. The root chakra is likewise associated with all the essentials necessary for grounding oneself, encompassing sustenance, water, refuge, security, and the emotional need for companionship, comfort, and personal safety. When all of these requirements are fulfilled, one experiences a sense of security, relaxation, and diminished concern.

What are the consequences of opening and blocking the Chakra?

The root chakra is correlated with the element of Earth, which is frequently recognized as the representation of being firmly rooted. Consequently, its primary function entails fostering a sense of grounding, security, and stability within an individual.

When the root chakra is in an open state, it permits the unimpeded and seamless flow of energy, thereby facilitating its efficient transmission to the subsequent six chakras in sequential order. One experiences a pervasive sense of tranquility, contentment, and satisfaction in regard to oneself and one's circumstances.

When equilibrium is achieved in the root chakra, one will not experience any issues associated with stress or anxiety, possess a positive self-perception, and maintain a sense of stability in one's life. You do not encounter any concerns regarding your survival, welfare, and stability, and experience a profound sense of safety and assurance across all significant facets of your life.

The blockage of the root chakra occurs when one experiences feelings of insecurity in any aspect of their life. Whenever you encounter concerns pertaining to your fundamental requirements, be it financial, residential, relational, or any other aspect that pertains to your sustenance, your root chakra experiences a state of imbalance. This misalignment leads to various issues, such as anxiety disorders, chronic stress, nightmares, as well as health complications, including digestive problems, disorders affecting the bladder and colon, and discomfort in the legs, back, and feet.

The occurrence of an energy blockage typically manifests as a sensation of intense apprehension and distress, which progressively escalates if not promptly addressed. The pervasive unease permeates your thoughts, eliciting a sense of uncertainty and self-doubt in all aspects of existence.

You exhibit challenges in maintaining focus on your tasks, demonstrate preoccupation with both genuine and imagined concerns, and operate within a consistent state of heightened activity. Your energy levels significantly decrease and you experience persistent feelings of exhaustion. Additionally, you face challenges in terms of your ability to engage in analytical reasoning and make well-founded judgments. Furthermore, you encounter difficulties in fostering a nourishing and balanced relationship with food, often oscillating between periods of extreme restriction and episodes of excessive consumption. If any of these issues resonate with you, it indicates an imbalanced state of the root chakra. Luckily, you can readily reinstate equilibrium by implementing the subsequent strategies.

Methods for Achieving Equilibrium in Your Root Chakra

Below are the proven techniques for healing your root chakra:

Crystal Healing

The root chakra is associated with the color red, therefore utilizing red crystals can be beneficial in maintaining its stability. To restore balance to this chakra, one may find benefit in employing Red Jasper, Obsidian, Bloodstone, or Red Carnelian. One may choose either of these stones and have it mounted in a pendant, necklace, or bracelet as a means to consistently stimulate the healing of their root chakra. One can also utilize the stone in its current state by investing 10 minutes daily to grasp it, concurrently envisioning the influx of vibrant crimson energy into the foundational core of the spine, steadily intensifying and illuminating with the passage of time.

While you mentally picture that, inhale deeply and envision the release of various forms of stress dissipating from your body. This straightforward technique, when performed consistently, gradually helps to rebalance the root chakra.

Root Chakra Mediation

This technique is a straightforward method of meditation that endeavors to reestablish equilibrium of energy within your root chakra. Assume a comfortable seated position with an upright posture, ensuring that your spine is aligned and your shoulders are held in a relaxed and expansive manner. Engage in a conscious effort to release tension in all muscle groups within your body, while simultaneously undertaking deep inhales through the nostrils and controlled exhalations through the mouth. Inhale deeply and consciously draw the breath deep into your abdomen, allowing it to evenly circulate and regulate throughout your entire physique. Please direct your focus towards the lower region of your spine and ascertain whether you are able to perceive any sensations of tension residing therein. Envision a gentle crimson radiance emanating from that location and contemplate its gradual expansion. Envision a gradual and comforting sensation in your coccyx region, as it warms, releases tension, and adopts a supple state. Continue to visualize an expanding red luminosity that gradually descends towards the earth, securely rooting you to its surface. Engaging in the activity for approximately 15 minutes will likely result in an increased sense of tranquility.

Consume the Appropriate Nourishment

Specific types of food can have a profound impact on the balance and vitality of your root chakra. It is important to incorporate protein-rich foods into your dietary intake, such as legumes, soy products, nuts, eggs, and leafy greens, as well as include red-hued foods such as cherries, strawberries, red peppers, and tomatoes. Staple vegetables like potatoes, garlic, onions, and beets also aid in restoring equilibrium to a disrupted root chakra.

Maintain Connectivity with the Earth

Engage in the practice of traversing uncovered terrain with your feet and exerting gentle pressure on it for a brief duration every day. Furthermore, partaking in earth-centric endeavors such as horticulture, sowing seeds, and tending to botanical life aids in the stabilization of one's root chakra.

Affirmations

An affirmation is a statement that you wholeheartedly endorse. It has the potential to produce positive, negative, or neutral outcomes. When an individual consciously asserts an idea within their cognition, their mind assimilates and subsequently fosters corresponding thoughts to manifest congruous occurrences in their reality.

In order to cultivate a sense of optimism, contentment, and success in life, it is imperative to nurture oneself with constructive positive affirmations. The aforementioned statement also pertains to the regulation of your root chakra. Presented here are a selection of affirmations that, if recited with unwavering conviction on a twice-daily basis, can effectively reinstate equilibrium within one's being.

I experience a sense of safety, stability, and rootedness.

I expel tension through exhalation and draw tranquility into my being through inhalation.

All of my safety requirements have been satisfactorily fulfilled.

I am in good health, and I am content with the richness of my life.

I am fully grounded to the terrestrial realm, finding solace in the pervasive embrace of the cosmos.

It is imperative to engage in consistent practice of these exercises in order to quickly achieve favorable outcomes. Now, we shall proceed to deliberate upon the second chakra in the forthcoming chapter.

Healing The Third Chakra

The Manipura chakra, also known as the solar plexus, is situated in the vicinity of the lower rib cage and upper abdomen, and is symbolized by the hue of yellow. This particular chakra is frequently linked to avian creatures and the act of flying, as it represents the initial energy center that facilitates our departure from the astral body and facilitates an enhanced connection with individuals, locations, and objects. From a physical standpoint, this chakra is linked to the musculature system, the digestive apparatus, our overall metabolic activity, and our nervous system.

In order to grasp the concept of the third chakra, it is imperative to discern its hierarchical position above the other two foundational chakras, which primarily pertain to individual survival. The third chakra pertains to the notion of self-acceptance, confidence, and interpersonal connectivity, making it the initial chakra concerned with these aspects. It represents a departure from the self-centric pursuit of personal pleasure and survival concerns, and a shift towards the values of communal harmony and companionship.

When the third chakra is adequately structured, we experience a sense of harmony in our capacity to establish meaningful connections with others and demonstrate adeptness in self-organization. When an obstruction or imbalance occurs in this particular chakra, it gives rise to significant challenges regarding our capacity to collaborate effectively or perform optimally within any collective scenario.

This may present itself in the form of challenges in navigating hierarchical structures, difficulty establishing social connections, feelings of anger, and a sense of frustration.

Fundamentally, this particular chakra assumes the role of governing our sense of self-worth and self-assurance as a member of society. If one experiences a state of discontentment or disillusionment with oneself, it inherently influences one's ability to connect with others and subsequently fosters feelings of resentment.

Associated fragrances: Marigold, cinnamon, and carnation.

Herbs that are associated with this include lemon balm and goldenseal.

The glandular system in question comprises the gallbladder, liver, and spleen.

Musical note: E

Phonetic representation of the chakra sound: The vowel sound 'O' can be pronounced as in words such as top, pop, or dollop.

Element: Fire

Healing gemstones: Golden topaz, tiger's eye, amber, golden calcite, pure gold, and citrine.

Color: Yellow

Healing exercises:

Kundalini yoga, specifically emphasizing the boat pose.

Engaging in rhythmic bodily movements and vibrations, particularly with a focus on swaying of the pelvis.

Healing foods:

Any objects or substances that possess a yellow hue, such as maize, legumes such as split peas, and certain varieties of beans.

Examples of grains and fiber-rich foods include whole wheat, granola, and whole grain.

Gentle herbal infusions, specifically those infused with peppermint and mint varieties.

How to achieve equilibrium within the root chakra

Eat root vegetables. Peel or dice freshly procured fruits, vegetables, or herbs. Bake bread. Establish routine. Retire to bed at an early hour. Wake up early. Perform a thorough cleaning and organizational overhaul of your residence. Make a charitable contribution or offer previously unused possessions for redistribution. Engage in recycling by sorting and repurposing items such as cans, bottles, boxes, and bags. Practice calming movement. Engage in the activities of walking, practicing yoga, or participating in Tai Chi. Walk barefoot. Connect with nature. Exercise options: jogging, aerobics, martial arts, kickboxing. Embark on cultivating a compact garden. Perform yard work. Obtain the services of a skilled masseuse/masseur for a professional therapeutic massage experience. Enroll in a support group. Please attempt the subsequent asanas: mountain/ prayer, tree.

THE SACRAL

Located beneath the navel region, the color orange is associated with fostering emotional equilibrium.

The attainment of equilibrium in the sacral chakra would result in elegant body movements and enhanced emotional discernment. It would bestow upon you the capability to gracefully adapt to circumstances and derive pleasure from the nuances of life. One could equally foster their own well-being and that of others, utilizing their intuition to establish the suitable limits. Alternatively, one could choose to reside ardently, engrossed in the pursuit of artistic endeavors and the realization of personal aspirations.

Should the prevailing energy be hindered, one's emotions may impede the process of self-discovery and hinder the cultivation of compassion. The failure to mobilize this emotional energy can lead to preoccupation, dependence, or profound apprehension. Another consequence that may arise is the manifestation of inadequate physical, mental, or emotional boundaries. A cautionary note: exerting force against the obstacle, rather than leaning into it, will only contribute to the depletion of energy resources. Persistent occurrences of depression or fatigue are associated with a significant disparity and necessitate careful treatment.

The second chakra is responsible for the maintenance and functioning of various internal organs and their corresponding systems. Encompassed within this category are the reproductive and sexual organs, urinary system, and lower intestines, along with the lower back and hips. An asymmetry can give rise to dysfunction or discomfort in any of these regions, alongside sciatic nerve pain. In the case of females, an irregular menstruation pattern or discomfort associated with it can be indicative of a pronounced hormonal imbalance.

Techniques For Achieving Equilibrium In The Sacral Chakra

Observe the rising or setting of the sun. Take a seat adjacent to a substantial aqueous expanse. Stroll amidst the rainfall. Consume an ample amount of rejuvenating water. Unwind on a rocking chair or porch swing. Employ deliberate, unhurried actions. Consider engaging in activities such as practicing Tai Chi, Yin Yoga, or engaging in walking meditation. Go camping. Arrange a dinner gathering with acquaintances. Attend a musical performance, cultural event, public gathering, or outdoor recreational venue. Indulge in a weekend retreat. Consider paying a visit to a wellness retreat or a boutique inn for a rejuvenating experience. Engage in the process of implementing the principles of Feng Shui to achieve a transformative redesign of your living space. Acquire fresh beddings and towels. Utilize candles, incense, or oils. Arrange floral arrangements or botanical specimens throughout the interior of your residence. Adorn your living area with fine artwork. Indulge in the melodious tunes of soothing, captivating music. Indulge in the enchantment of a romantic literary work, cinematic masterpiece, or theatrical production. Engage in the process of emotional catharsis or emotional regulation. Set clear demarcations within interpersonal connections. Participate in a 12-step program designed to address addictive behaviors. Please consider practicing the subsequent yoga postures: forward fold, cobra pose, and pigeon pose.

THE SOLAR PLEXUS

Superior to the abdominal region, characterized by the color yellow, denotes dynamism and objective.

The attainment of equilibrium in the solar plexus region fosters a profound sense of meaning and direction in one's existence. In addition to possessing the physical stamina required to navigate daily tasks, you would also exhibit the cognitive fortitude and resolve essential for tackling unforeseen obstacles and accomplishing objectives. If one possesses self-discipline, an amiable disposition, and a sense of assurance, one has achieved a certain equilibrium. Consistently executing everyday responsibilities instills a surplus of vitality within your inner being.

If progress seems stagnant in one's life, it is probable that an incongruity exists within the solar plexus. The initial indication of being in a state of stagnation is the incapacity to direct one's attention inwardly. Your energy appears dispersed, lacking a discernible central focus. An impaired personal reputation or compromised personal motives also demonstrate the same characteristics. An imbalance may manifest itself through a range of manifestations: exhibiting aggressive behavior, seeking solace in addictive tendencies, forming unhealthy attachments, or exhibiting a complete refusal to take action.

The solar plexus, in its intermediary state, regulates the state of equilibrium within the physical being. The key areas of emphasis revolve around the gastrointestinal system and the vertebral column. Therefore, any physiological ailments within the peritoneal cavity can be attributed to a state of imbalance. Some dysfunctions that should be monitored include issues pertaining to digestion or elimination, decreased appetite, eating disorders, diabetes, and arthritis. Additionally, the presence of excess weight or feelings of fatigue can also serve as indications of an underlying imbalance.

The Obstruction Or Hindrance Of The Sacral Chakra

The sacral chakra may experience various factors that can lead to its blockage. Instances of sexual abuse, including acts such as rape or assault, are clearly recognized as a prominent factor leading to the development of an obstructed sacral chakra. If this is found to be the contributing factor to the obstruction, it would entail undertaking a protracted and rigorous endeavor centered around addressing the sacral chakra.

An obstruction of the sacral chakra may also occur when an initial relationship deteriorates in a highly dramatic manner. In the event that a woman engages in her initial sexual relationship and encounters instances of betrayal or emotional mistreatment, it may result in an obstruction of the sacral chakra.

There are numerous factors that can contribute to the obstruction of the sacral chakra. As an illustration, in cases where parents possess unconventional inhibitions towards a wholesome perspective on sexuality, their influence can potentially impede the energy flow within the sacral chakra during the formative years of a child. Frequently, this is a phenomenon that has been inherited across successive generations, and the puritanical perspectives on sexuality have, in numerous instances, given rise to a pervasive cultural trend encompassing challenges associated with the sacral chakra. In contemporary times, albeit the increased openness and acceptance of sexuality within Western societies, the enduring influence of puritanical heritage remains prevalent. The puritan perspective on life extends beyond the manifestation of sexual desires as well. It also hinders the overall experience of pleasure. The pervasive influence of the puritanical perspective on our mindset may often go unnoticed, yet it undeniably exerts a significant impact on American culture. This influence has the effect of instilling in women the perception that pleasure and enjoyment are inherently immoral or impure. When an idea or notion is experienced and internalized rather than solely cognitively understood, it possesses a greater potential to wield influence, becoming deeply ingrained within the subconscious. Consequently, this may lead to the occurrence of an obstruction within the sacral chakra.

The proliferation of explicit material merits significant consideration and poses a challenging subject for women to discuss. The prevalence of easily accessible pornography on the internet is leading to the obstruction of the sacral chakra among women. While it is not implied that women ought to abstain from consuming pornography, it should be noted that engaging in such activities can potentially lead to disruptions or imbalances in the sacral chakra. The primary peril arising from this phenomenon is the potential development of an excessive preoccupation with sexuality.

Additionally, it can foster an excessive inclination towards fantastical thinking. Engaging in an idealized existence can impede the establishment of genuine intimate connections, leading to the formulation of unattainable expectations borne out of excessive indulgence in fantasy and pornography.

Surprisingly, pornography has the ability to diminish the vitality of the sacred energy center known as the sacral chakra. Excessive exposure to explicit content can potentially diminish a woman's inclination towards sexuality or the pursuit of pleasure. Nothing seems to satisfy. Exercise caution when accessing or engaging with this material.

Indications of an Obstruction in the Sacral Chakra

As previously indicated in the preceding two sections, a hindrance to the sacral chakra commonly presents itself in contrasting manners. One possible alternative phrasing in a formal tone could be: "An initial manifestation of an obstructed sacral chakra involves a diminished perception of the surrounding environment." You shall encounter a lack of inspiration and the inability to derive pleasure. You may observe a significant decline in your sexual appetites, possibly resulting in a complete absence of any such desires.

This emotional apathy has the potential to extend to any realm wherein the enjoyment of senses is a fundamental aspect of existence. In the event of a significant obstruction in the sacral chakra, one may experience an inability to derive pleasure from the act of consuming food and beverages. Food may possibly lose its appeal and flavor, leading to a lack of pleasure and diminished appetite, even though consumption may be motivated primarily by the need for sustenance.

A hinderance in the sacral chakra can also influence the functioning of the root chakra, thereby potentially instigating feelings of apprehension and unease. One might discover oneself refraining from engaging in intimate relationships with individuals of the female gender. Occasionally, diminished self-regard in terms of one's perception of personal sexual appeal might ensue. Additionally, one could partake in excessive consumption of food as a means to fulfill one's own prophecy, whereby the subconscious mind endeavors to diminish one's sexual allure.

Insufficient self-esteem can cause women with an obstructed sacral chakra to engage in unfavorable and harmful relationships, or potentially refrain from entering relationships altogether. These relationships will be characterized by a sense of fear and jealousy, which stem from the feelings of insecurity and inadequate self-worth associated with a blocked sacral chakra. The occurrence of depression often accompanies the prolonged obstruction of the sacral chakra.

The manifestation of physical symptoms associated with sexuality and reproduction can be viewed as a natural consequence of an impediment in the sacral chakra. Frequently, they serve to fulfill the purpose of pretexts for evading sexual relationships. Urinary tract infections are likely to occur frequently. Sexual dysfunction, including erectile dysfunction, frequently occurs in males who have an obstructed sacral chakra, along with associated difficulties in sexual performance. Females may experience vaginal dryness or encounter other issues related to menstruation, while both genders may face complications with fertility.

Additional physical manifestations of an obstructed sacral chakra encompass the presence of urinary and renal calculi, anomalies within the female reproductive system such as cysts, infrequent bowel movements, and discomfort in the lumbar region.

If an individual's sacral chakra is obstructed, they may discover themselves excessively allocating their time and energy to indulging in fantasies. This may encompass sexual fantasies, frequently accompanied by excessive engagement in self-stimulation. This might impede your capacity to develop and experience fulfilling sexual relationships with other women. In addition to sexual fantasies, women who experience an obstructed sexual chakra may encounter a phenomenon where their active engagement in a fantasy leads to a depletion of creativity in their actual lives.

As previously mentioned, it is imperative to remain vigilant for any indications of an imbalanced sacral chakra. The indications of this condition entail an excessive allocation of energy towards pursuits of pleasure and addictive tendencies. Your life is in a state of imbalance when you partake in these activities, such as consuming alcohol excessively every evening until reaching intoxication, dedicating all of your leisure time and financial resources to gambling, displaying an extreme preoccupation with food and eating, or exhibiting an excessive preoccupation with sex. These indicators necessitate your efforts in rectifying and restoring equilibrium to the sacral chakra.

Foods that nourish the Sacral Chakra

Consuming appropriate dietary choices can facilitate the equilibrium and restoration of the sacral chakra. Thankfully, the abundance of nourishing dietary options found within the realm of the natural world can provide support in the activation and restoration of the sacral chakra. Furthermore, these dietary options frequently possess advantages for the foundational chakra, affording the opportunity to concurrently nurture and harmonize both. Furthermore, it should be noted that a significant proportion of these food items boast a remarkable nutritional profile. When selecting foods for this purpose, please consider the color orange.

Consuming vegetables such as carrots and sweet potatoes can contribute to the balancing of both the root and sacral chakras. This can be attributed to their vibrant deep orange hues, coupled with their inherent status as underground vegetables that foster a sense of grounding and security.

Additional food options that contribute to the restoration of the sacral chakra equilibrium encompass oranges, orange juice, orange peppers, mangos, orange cantaloupes, peaches, and apricots. Salmon constitutes a highly commendable source of protein, possessing the capacity to aid in the balancing and alignment of both the root and sacral chakras. Consuming beef steak can additionally contribute to the enhancement of sexual vitality. Additionally, there have been reports suggesting that almonds and walnuts possess the potential to facilitate the healing of the sacral chakra. Given that the sacral chakra embodies the essence of water, ensuring hydration by consuming sufficient quantities of pure water can effectively sustain the balance of the sacral chakra. An alternative option to consider would be incorporating vitamin C supplements into your regimen.

Essential Oils for the Sacral Chakra

The utilization of piquant essential oils can be advantageous for the sacral chakra, which is connected to sensuality and gratification. Sandalwood, known for its efficacy in balancing the root chakra, also confers advantageous effects on the sacral chakra. An alternate option would be to utilize the essence of orange oil. To promote sexual arousal, numerous women attest to the efficacy of ylang-ylang, which is also purported to possess tranquilizing properties. This will assist in promoting a state of relaxation and receptiveness to experiencing pleasure. Clary sage possesses subtle spiciness and has been noted for its ability to induce relaxation, allowing for an enhanced awareness of one's sensuality. It proves to be of great utility, especially for women of advanced age. Additionally, it is prudent to take into consideration the utilization of essential oils and the application of lower back massage techniques.

Hues designated for the Sacral Chakra

The sacral chakra exhibits a strong correlation with a profound hue of vibrant orange. One can enhance their sensual energies by immersing oneself in an environment adorned with the color orange. Please take into consideration the option of incorporating orange sheets, pillowcases, or bedspreads as an addition to the bedroom. Incorporate orange cushions within your designated space for meditation. One can enhance their sexual energy by adorning oneself with garments in vivid shades of orange.

Using Crystals to Balance the Sacral Chakra

Carnelian is the primary crystal that is commonly associated with the sacral chakra. When this remarkable stone is polished, its precise vibrant deep orange hues serve to stimulate the sacral chakra. Kindly contemplate adorning your bedroom with carnelian stones. Gently cradle them within your palms, either for the purpose of experiencing their presence or during moments of meditation, and allow yourself to sense their energetic essence as you internalize it. Acquire a carnelian pendant or necklace to adorn your person, thereby enhancing your sensual experience.

Amber is likewise an excellent crystal to utilize in order to harmonize and activate the sacral chakra. Additionally, there is a convergence with the solar plexus chakra, whereby the utilization of amber can be achieved by procuring jewelry crafted from amber and adorning oneself with it.

Goldstone is a deep hue of orange crystal that exhibits the additional capability of facilitating the harmonization of the sacral chakra. Additionally, sunstone, tiger's eye, and citrine may be employed for such purposes. Nevertheless, it should be observed that these crystals predominantly display a yellow hue and wield a more substantial influence over the solar plexus chakra. To conclude, the carnelian stone is the principal crystal recommended for effective healing and balancing of the sacral chakra.

Contemplative Practices for Nurturing the Sacral Energy Center

Meditation will play a significant role in facilitating the healing process of the sacral chakra. In order to facilitate the healing of the sacral chakra, it is recommended to adorn the meditation space with vibrant hues of orange. If it is feasible for you to engage in daytime meditation, particularly during the morning hours, I recommend ensuring that the room is equipped with open windows that permit ample sunlight to illuminate the space. The meditation practice for the sacral chakra will adhere to the fundamental approach outlined in the preceding chapter. Commence by assuming a seated position in easy pose and gently close your eyes, taking deliberate and rhythmic breaths. In the practice of meditation, it is advisable to slightly lower the chin in order to facilitate the expansion of the spine, thereby enhancing the circulation of energy when focusing specifically on the sacral chakra. Certain women also recommend practicing meditation unclothed or with minimal attire while focusing on the restoration of the sacral chakra, as this allows for the heightened awareness of sensuality permeating the entirety of the body. If one feels at ease and is afforded the necessary privacy, it can greatly enhance the overall encounter.

Commence the process by visualizing a radiant white disc positioned in front of you. Inhale and retain your breath for a duration of three to five seconds. Begin observing the disk as it initiates a gradual rotation. Observe the disc's gradual transition into an orange hue as it undergoes rotation. Envision the progressive infusion of the orange hue within the rotating disk, as its speed intensifies over time, engendering amplified levels of energy. Now, experience the ingress of the ball of luminosity into your being, ascending gradually and acquiring a more profound and radiant hue of orange as it progresses towards your root chakra. Continue to engage in mental imagery and envision the luminous disc gradually taking on a profound, vivid, and dynamic shade of orange. Now, envision its movement towards the area of your sacral chakra, situated below the navel.

Direct your focus towards the sacral chakra region and the area encompassing your genital region. Maintain a conscious state of awareness encompassing all the sensory experiences, with a specific focus on acknowledging the emergence of heat sensations. Additionally, one may envision the diffusion of radiant, luminous orange energy enveloping the region surrounding the breasts. Embrace healthy sexuality by wholeheartedly engaging in it while exercising natural restraint, without any inhibition. The contemplative exercises will assist you in reaching this stage in your journey.

Consider the scenario of the orange disk ascending towards your cerebral cortex. This approach will contribute to the enhancement of your creativity, fostering constructive and non-obsessive indulgence in healthy imaginative thoughts. You may conclude the meditation at this juncture.

Positive Declarations for the Sacral Energy Center

Employing positive affirmations can aid in restoring equilibrium within the sacral chakra, thereby facilitating the eradication of detrimental conditioning associated with sexuality and sensuality.

I am able to engage in sexual activity without compromising my personal safety.

- I exude an aura of sexuality and sensuality. • I emanate a strong sense of sexuality and sensuality. • I project an image of being both sensual and sexually attractive. • I embody an air of sensuality and sexual appeal.

I grant myself the permission to experience a sense of ease.

I am capable of experiencing enjoyment without experiencing any sense of wrongdoing.

• I possess the capacity to experience and derive pleasure from all the joys and delights that life has to present.

• My capacity to derive immense pleasure from fine dining experiences is significantly enhanced.

• I am drawn to women who share similar mindsets and possess a strong sense of well-being in their attitudes towards sexuality.

• I am capable of engaging in healthy expressions of my sexuality.

I derive pleasure from the various pursuits that life presents, while keeping myself from being engulfed by them.

I am profoundly in touch with my emotions, yet they do not overpower me.

- I possess robust and harmonized emotions.

- I am experiencing a sense of tranquility and serenity.

- I possess inherent creative abilities.

I possess a profound sense of creativity and derive immense joy from showcasing and disseminating it to others.

I enable the full expression of my emotions to permeate every fiber of my being.

- I feel at ease with my physical appearance. • I am content with the way my body looks and feels. • I am satisfied with the condition and appearance of my body. • I find myself in a state of acceptance and contentment regarding my physical form.

I experience a heightened sense of sensuality within my physical being.

- Sexual activity is a secure and meaningful way for me to foster profound connections.

Root Chakra Meditations

The initial chakra point is the root chakra, recognized as Muladhara, derived from the term 'Mula' denoting root and 'Dhara' signifying support or foundation. The foundational chakra facilitates a profound sense of emotional stability and personal well-being. It establishes a profound connection between your spiritual energy and the Earth, fostering a sense of tranquility with regards to your fundamental human needs, namely financial stability, sustenance, and abode. The hue that is linked to this particular chakra is red, symbolizing attributes such as vitality, resilience, affection, and passion. It can be found situated within the coccyx, which corresponds to the anatomical region known as the tailbone in the spinal column. When your root chakra achieves equilibrium, you experience a sense of serenity and harmony in both your existence and your connection with the terrestrial realm. In situations pertaining to your essential needs for survival, you will attain a state of tranquility.

Nevertheless, in the event of an imbalance in your chakra, you are likely to experience frequent sensations of stress and anxiety due to the correlation between fear and the instinct to ensure one's survival. It evokes a sense of vitality, albeit in a negative manner. This phenomenon has the potential to induce unfounded apprehension and elicit emotional reactions such as insecurity, avarice, impatience, anger, and irascibility in individuals. From a physical standpoint, you may experience gastrointestinal disturbances, discomfort in the hips, urinary difficulties, problems with the lower back, and an overall sense of exhaustion.

To achieve equilibrium in your chakra system and reinstate your body to its former state, implementing a modest dietary adjustment can exert a profound impact on your physical well-being and the fundamental stability of the root chakra. If you are regularly consuming a substantial amount of nutritionally detrimental substances, it is advisable to modify your dietary patterns by embracing a healthier and more nourishing food intake. In addition to its positive impact on the root chakra, the practice also imparts preventive benefits against ailments and maintains overall health by detoxifying the body. Certain crimson-hued food items, such as strawberries, tomatoes, and red peppers, possess the ability to facilitate the unblocking of the root chakra. Engaging in physical activity or practicing yoga can serve as alternative methods to facilitate the clearing of chakra blockages. Walking without shoes can facilitate a stronger connection with the earth, thereby enhancing the sensation of being firmly rooted. Meditation is widely recognized as the most efficacious method for accessing and unblocking chakra points. Provided herein are several guidelines and techniques to conduct a proper and focused meditation session specifically targeting this particular chakra.

Unique meditation program designed to facilitate deep-rooted harmony in the foundational energy center

The initial step you should undertake is to ensure your comfort. Position yourself in a seated posture, with your legs crossed and your spine and shoulders aligned in an upright and dignified manner. Assume a seated position with your hands placed upon your knees, ensuring that the palms are turned upwards. Alternatively, you may opt to adopt the mudra hand position, by positioning your hands on your knees with the palms facing upwards, while forming a circular shape with your fingers (in a similar manner as the 'okay' hand gesture).

Please allocate a brief period of time to unwind your muscles and physicality, directing your concentration towards your respiration during the inhalation and exhalation process. Do not heed the thoughts or mental disturbances that arise within your mind. Direct your attention solely to your own person, disregarding any other matters. Please refrain from dwelling on your pending tasks or contemplating your evening meal, as such thoughts may significantly disrupt your concentration. Kindly direct your attention towards various regions of your physique for a brief period. Unwind the tension in your facial muscles, arms, and abdominal region. Experience the sensation of tingling as you allow your body to become devoid of feeling. Gradually redirect your focus towards your breath. Observe the manner in which your thoracic region elevates and descends with each inhalation and exhalation. Gently permit your eyes to close with a sensation akin to drifting into slumber.

Commence the process of inhaling and exhaling at a slow and profound pace, while endeavoring to sustain a consistent and fluid respiratory rhythm. Upon Inhalation, observe the descent of the air into your abdominal region, followed by its ascent through the nasal passages during exhalation. Inhale and exhale deliberately, ensuring profound breaths, prior to directing your attention towards the position of the root chakra, which resides at the foundational point of your spine, specifically where your tailbone is situated.

Breathe in deeply and tighten the muscles located between the pubic bone and the tailbone, actively activating the Mula Bandha. You are bringing the perineum closer to the base of the chakra system. Direct your focus towards the sensation of the Mula Bandha as the inhalation gracefully enters and the muscles engage. Take a momentary pause of one to two seconds before gradually relinquishing the Mula Bandha and easing the tension in your muscles. Please reiterate this action by further tensing and compressing the muscles; notice the elongation of your spine as it elevates your posture while exerting downward pressure on your legs and feet. Release your grip after a brief interval and allow your muscles to once again attain a state of relaxation. Continue the aforementioned activity for a duration of three to five minutes, or for a period that is deemed appropriate. If you find yourself at ease with this muscle contraction, endeavor to gradually intensify it as you proceed with the remaining duration of the meditation.

Resume a controlled and intentional breath pattern, while envisioning a crimson radiance emanating from the base of your spine, without engaging in the practice of Mula Bandha. The radiance is steadily increasing, evoking a sense of comfort and tranquility within you. Experience the presence of the root chakra, perceive any bodily sensations, such as a gentle warmth or subtle tingling, specifically located in the region of the tailbone. Kindly and delicately immerse yourself in the sensations for a brief period while taking slow and profound breaths.

Gradually, begin to open your eyes, allowing them to acclimate to the surrounding light while gently blinking several times. Remain present in that moment and reflect on the impact of this meditation on your state of being before continuing with the rest of your day.

Utilizing positive affirmations can also be highly advantageous in the process of healing your root chakra. You have the liberty to reiterate them as frequently as you desire, whether vocally or mentally. The timing for reciting these statements is not limited to any specific time of day; however, it is pivotal to recognize that reciting them before or after engaging in meditation, or promptly upon awakening and commencing your preparations for the day, tends to yield heightened effectiveness. Presented here are several statements that possess the potential to restore balance to your chakra system and instill a profound sense of assurance in your existence, irrespective of your current level of belief in their veracity. Your assertion is aimed at actualizing their veracity.

I maintain a profound connection with both the terrestrial realm and the celestial domain."

I consistently prioritize my safety and well-being."

I have strong admiration for myself and my physical being."

I possess a robust financial footing for my future, leaving me unencumbered by any concerns or anxieties."

I am in good health both physically and emotionally."

When an individual is undergoing an activated root chakra, they may encounter a sensation of warmth emanating from their physique, particularly concentrated in the vicinity of the lower region of the spinal column. You will experience a sense of stability and harmonious connection with the earth, which may enhance the sensitivity of your feet. You will gradually experience a sense of comfort towards matters that previously caused you anxiety. In order to activate your chakra points, it is necessary to release any inhibiting emotions, such as negative sentiments, financial burdens, and personal insecurities. Although it may initially appear challenging, once you acquire proficiency in managing life's complexities and experience a sense of tranquility, genuine happiness will be realized.

Please ensure that you allocate an adequate amount of time for the purpose of engaging in proper meditation. It may present challenges to allocate a portion of your daily schedule for an activity that may not appear significant; nevertheless, in order to attain equilibrium in all your chakras, concentration is imperative. The recommended duration for the meditation you will be engaging in is approximately thirty to sixty minutes.

Locate a suitable location for your meditation practice. Ideally, the preferable location would possess qualities of calmness, tranquility, and absence of noise. You desire an undisturbed state whilst engaged in the act of meditation. One also desires the ability to maintain a comfortable seated position for a considerable duration. It may be prudent to consider venturing to a location that bears symbolic connotations to the specific chakra you are directing your attention towards. In this scenario, it would entail directing yourself towards an outdoor environment characterized by rocky terrain or mountainous landscapes.

To seek assistance in aligning one's thoughts with this particular chakra, various meditation tools and aids can be employed. Stones present a traditional illustration in this regard; the inherent energy encapsulated within the stone facilitates the enhancement, stimulation, and purification of the chakra's energy. The Root Chakra can be supported by employing stones such as red carnelian for purification and activation, red jasper for purification and equilibrium, bloodstone for purification and equilibrium, black tourmaline for purification and equilibrium, and obsidian for purification and equilibrium.

For optimal effectiveness of these stones, it is advisable to position them in proximity to the corresponding chakra that is experiencing imbalance. In this scenario, it would be advisable to position them in close proximity to your pelvic region. They can also be conveniently positioned throughout your residence or workplace, conveniently transported, or tastefully adorned as ornamental accessories.

Additional mindfulness tools that could provide support encompass fragrances and nourishment. Aromatherapy plays a beneficial role in the practice of meditation as it offers olfactory stimulation to enhance concentration and mental focus. In regards to the Root Chakra, suitable fragrances encompass botanical oils that emanate floral and earthy aromas, such as sandalwood, patchouli, myrrh, ylang-ylang, and rosemary.

Additionally, there are certain food items that possess the capability to facilitate chakra healing and can be seamlessly integrated into your meditation practice. The aforementioned items comprise beans, soy, meat, tofu, rainbow chard, eggs, parsnips, and beets.

After arranging your meditation aids, it is time to commence the practice of meditation. To accomplish this, assume a comfortable seated position on the floor and gently cross your legs, utilizing a cushion or alternative support if desired. Please ensure proper posture by maintaining an upright position and allowing your arms to hang comfortably.

You'll want to first start out by clearing your mind of everything, especially negative emotions. It is imperative that you possess the capacity to concentrate your complete attention on this particular chakra.

Next, mentally envision the chakra within its designated position. In relation to the Root Chakra, it is advisable to engage in the visualization of a crimson orb of light located at the foundational point of the spine, engaged in a descending rotational motion. Direct your attention towards regulating the flow of energy within this specific chakra.

In order to facilitate concentration, it is advised to employ a specific mantra associated with each chakra to be reiterated while engaging in meditation. The mantra associated with the Root Chakra is "LAM."

Reiterating affirmations for every chakra is of utmost significance. For the Root Chakra, affirm, "I am inherently linked to the Earth; I embody steadfastness and resilience."

By means of diligent practice and the application of these techniques, you will expeditiously attain the skill to proficiently harmonize and manage your Root Chakra.

Engaging in meditation for the fundamental energy center known as the Root Chakra, utilizing the sacred syllable "Lam".

An excessive root chakra can give rise to a multitude of issues. It has the potential to induce a heightened sense of materialism or promiscuity in individuals. It has the potential to induce feelings of insecurity and unwarranted anxieties as well. To ensure proper maintenance of the root chakra, the appropriate approach would involve achieving equilibrium through morning walks or jogs, or engaging in regular physical activity to promote overall bodily well-being. Maintaining a state of bodily relaxation and adopting correct posture can also be advantageous. When preparing to engage in meditation, it is recommended to maintain a stance with feet positioned at a width equivalent to the shoulders, while moderately bending the knees and leaning the lower body slightly forward. Sustaining this posture for a brief duration is advised. Following a brief period, the body attains a state of preparedness for meditation, at which point one may assume a seated position with crossed legs and hands placed gently upon the knees. The hands can be either open or with the thumb and index finger gently pressed together, depending on whichever position promotes relaxation and enhances concentration. After completing the necessary preparations, commence the process of visualizing the chakra situated at the base of your spine and proceed to relax. It is advisable to consider employing the aforementioned recommendations, such as mentally envisioning a flourishing flower as a symbolic representation of the base chakra. Keep the image in your head while breathing slowly and deeply until you begin to feel refreshed. The fundamental energy center known as the root chakra is associated with the earth element and is distinguished by the hue of red. The utilization of specific gemstones, such as jasper or garnet, has the potential to facilitate the restoration of equilibrium within your root chakra. The mantra for the root chakra is enunciated as "Lahm," and it is important to ensure that the muscles are maximally relaxed during exhalation if this mantra is employed.

What Are Chakras? A Detailed Understanding

As previously mentioned, the term "chakra" derives from the Sanskrit word "wheel". In the event that one had the capability to perceive each chakra, what would be witnessed is an uninterrupted, cyclic movement of an energetic wheel. The chakras within the human body originate from the sacrum and ascend towards the crown of the head, aligning with the central axis of the spinal column. Moreover, they exhibit a symmetrical pattern extending both anteriorly and posteriorly, permeating the entirety of the physical form. The image displayed below depicts the seven chakras:

As previously mentioned, energy resonates at varying velocities. More specifically, each individual chakra is characterized by its own unique frequency of vibration and rotational motion. The initial chakra, referred to as the root chakra, exhibits the most sluggish rotation, while the seventh chakra, commonly identified as the crown chakra, manifests the swiftest rotation.

The color provided in the image above, which serves as a complementary hue, alongside a variety of crystals with targeted purposes, effectively activates and energizes all of the chakras. The hues of the rainbow encompass the chakra colors, which include shades of red, orange, yellow, green, blue, indigo, and violet. Please bear in mind that the brightness of the wheels may be influenced by various factors, including but not limited to physical conditions, individual development, energy levels, disease, and stress.

A perpetual equilibrium among your chakras bestows upon you a profound state of welfare and fosters optimal physical well-being.

Regrettably, in the event of chakra blockages or an inability to achieve equilibrium, there is a noticeable decrease in their efficacy. In the event of such circumstances, individuals may experience fatigue, lethargy, despondency, or a general sense of being unsettled. Furthermore, in addition to the physiological symptoms resulting from disrupted bodily functions, the mental and cognitive processes can be impacted by any imbalance in the chakras. In the event that one of your chakras becomes obstructed or falls out of alignment, it gives rise to a preoccupation with negative attitudes, uncertainty, anxiety, delay, and related manifestations.

Regrettably, excessive opening of the chakras can culminate in the surging energy detrimentally disrupting the seamless functioning of your physical being. Alternatively, in instances where your chakras become closed or blocked, this impedes the unhindered circulation of energy, thereby giving rise to potential ailments.

When an individual responds to life experiences by suppressing their emotions and inhibiting the innate energy flow, this can have negative repercussions on the growth and maturation of their chakras. When individuals suppress their experiences, it can lead to the distortion and obstruction of their chakras. When the chakra system is in a state of proper functionality, all chakras will be activated and rotate in a clockwise manner, facilitating the assimilation of the energies sourced from the universe.

The occurrence of any disparities in the functioning of your chakras may lead to detrimental physical and emotional consequences for your overall well-being. As previously alluded to, one can realign their chakras and facilitate the augmentation of energy circulation within them.

In order to facilitate this, we will be examining specific yoga postures, meditation methods, crystals, and various other techniques that can be employed to activate, harmonize, and restore equilibrium to your seven chakras, thereby augmenting holistic wellness.

Techniques for the Alignment, Healing, and Harmonization of Individual Chakras

Root Chakra (Muladhara)

Element: Earth

Sound: Lam

Color: Red

Position: The region situated at the base of the coccyx or spine

Corresponding gland: Adrenal

The Muladhara, referred to as the root chakra in Sanskrit, governs various aspects of an individual's life, including family connections, sense of belonging, self-preservation, and cautiousness. This location serves as the repository for all your earliest recollections, encompassing the satisfaction or insufficiency of your fundamental requirements.

When this chakra is blocked or imbalanced, you become needy, low self-esteemed, and sometimes, having self-destructive behaviors. When the root chakra is harmonized, one experiences a sense of self-assurance and resilience, capable of independent existence and self-sufficiency.

Indications of Disharmony within the Root Chakra

The occurrence of physical disharmony within your root chakra manifests as issues pertaining to your lower limbs, coccyx, anus, immune system, prostate gland, and reproductive system. Additional indications of potential imbalances within your root chakra encompass symptoms such as anguish in the knees, afflictions related to arthritis, disturbances in eating patterns, sciatic nerve discomfort, as well as irregularities in bowel movements.

Emotional disturbances encompass sensations that impact fundamental requirements for survival, including lodging, financial means, nourishment, and capacity to meet life's essential necessities.

Indications of Equilibrium in the Base Chakra

When the root chakra attains equilibrium, individuals experience a sense of interconnectedness, stability, groundedness, and security.

Insights Derived from the Root Chakra

Self-preservation is the entitlement to occupy one's current position.

Methods to Activate the Fundamental Chakra

The Tree Pose

This posture necessitates assuming a stance where your feet are positioned at a distance equal to the width of your hips. This position affords you a secure foundation. Upon exhalation, gently bend your knees, relax your pelvic area, and activate your thigh muscles. Place the sole of your right foot on the inner area of your left calf or thigh, while simultaneously lowering your tailbone and activating the thigh of your supporting leg to uphold a stable posture.

As you elevate your posture by extending the height of your head, exert downward force through the sole of your left foot. Inhale and exhale deeply five times while alternately changing positions. Embrace the force of gravity as it anchors you, all the while being conscious of the upward flow of energy along your spine.

Methods for Restoring the Balance of the Root Chakra

Fortunately, there exist several accessible and cost-free methods that are capable of restoring balance to your root chakra. Given that the root chakra is emblematic of one's stability and foundation, as well as being linked to the hue of red, presented below are a few methods for restoring and rejuvenating this vital energy center:

* Engage in prolonged bouts of barefoot ambulation

Incorporate red-colored produce like tomatoes, strawberries, red peppers, and beetroot into your diet, while also integrating flavorful spices on a regular basis.

If you have concerns regarding your financial situation, devise a savings strategy.

Exhibit your dance moves with confidence, disregarding the presence of spectators, and ensure that your hip movements are executed in a fitting manner.

Envision a crimson energy permeating the surrounding areas of your root chakra.

Auras, How To See Them

Aura can be defined as the electromagnetic emission and acoustic resonance exhibited by an object in response to external stimuli, such as the presence of surrounding illumination. This definition is a functional definition, and you will gain a deeper comprehension as we progress. It can be asserted that every entity within the cosmos is fundamentally a manifestation of vibratory energy. I would prefer not to regale you with lengthy anecdotes or convoluted jargon. Consult the dictionary for the term "aura" and you will find its definition as follows: a distinctive essence or ambience that emanates from an individual, location, or object.

What exactly does this aura consist of? May I inquire about the means by which I may observe them? May I pose a brief inquiry: What methodology can be employed to quantify the concept of beauty? How do you experience a profound sense of captivation when visiting an art gallery and encountering a piece of artwork that completely mesmerizes you? Would you be able to provide a thorough explanation?

What is the purpose of observing auras? While observing someone's aura, one can indeed discern their thoughts before such thoughts are articulated verbally. Deception can be detected with relative ease, as it tends to occur effortlessly. It is commonly asserted that individuals, particularly those within the tender age of five, possess the innate ability to perceive auras, thus suggesting that at some juncture in our lives, we too possessed such a capability.

What is the methodology through which we perceive and interpret auras?

It is not particularly remarkable; we have the capacity to perceive auras both visually and intuitively. Occasionally, one may observe the presence of a combination of oscillation frequencies within a specific spectrum that is perceptible to the human visual apparatus. One can observe auras by cultivating the ability to perceive auric energies and enhancing visual acuity to encompass a broader range of vibrational frequencies. Employing one's peripheral vision can prove advantageous for perceiving aura, while concurrently augmenting the brain's processing of visual sensations, thereby facilitating the development of communication and interaction between the cerebral hemispheres.

The Importance Of Restoring And Harmonizing The Chakras

Each of your chakras is positioned in such a way that it corresponds to particular physical dysfunctions and other ailments. Furthermore, each locus of vitality encapsulates your fortitudes on an affective and cognitive plane. Whenever a matter arises pertaining to our physical well-being, it subsequently gives rise to emotional vulnerability. Once you expel any lingering stagnant energies within your body promptly, these dysfunctions, along with any sensations of rigidity or constriction, will be alleviated.

Restoring the Equilibrium of the Chakras: "

Your emotional equilibrium will be replenished once you successfully dispel this stagnant energy. There exists a reciprocal correlation between the physical and mental aspects of your being. If one clings to particular emotions or fears, it will result in discernible limitations on a physical plane as well. Should you experience any degree of bodily stiffness or discomfort, alongside recurring fears or emotions, the act of perusing this literature ought to provide you with an elucidation regarding the chakra that may be obstructed or impacted by such manifestations.

The Crimson Chakra: As previously indicated, this particular chakra is located at the coccyx, situated at the lowermost part of the vertebral column. When imbalances manifest in this domain, they give rise to complications concerning the immune system, coccyx, lower extremities, and, in the case of males, the reproductive system and prostate gland. Individuals who experience a disparity in the functioning of their root chakra may exhibit symptoms such as constipation, the onset of eating disorders, and the manifestation of knee pain and arthritis.

Additionally, the presence of emotional imbalances arises when this particular chakra is in a state of disharmony, resulting in difficulties in fulfilling essential survival requirements such as sustenance, housing, and finances. When the root chakra achieves equilibrium, one will experience a sense of interconnectedness, nurturance, and rootedness within the realm of existence. This incident serves as a valuable reminder for us to acknowledge our place on this planet and actively engage with it.

The Sacral Chakra: Situated just below the umbilicus, this energetic center manifests issues pertaining to sexual functioning, the urinary system, renal health, as well as discomfort in the lumbar region, pelvis, and hip area. In the event of an imbalance in this particular chakra, one is prone to experiencing emotional challenges, including difficulties in forming committed relationships or partnerships, hindered expression of emotions, and a reduced capacity to unwind and derive pleasure from life's activities. Additionally, this method increases your susceptibility to addiction, as well as engenders concerns related to betrayal or instances of erectile dysfunction.

After attaining chakra realignment, you will regain the ability to effortlessly engage in creative pursuits, undertake crucial risks, and wholeheartedly devote yourself to significant responsibilities. You will experience a heightened sense of sociability, sensuality, and fervor towards life. One can acquire valuable insight from this disparity, namely the significance of according reverence to others.

The Solar Plexus Chakra: Situated a few inches above the navel, this energetic focal point can give rise to the subsequent conditions when its equilibrium is disturbed: ailments affecting the colon, gallbladder, or pancreas, as well as gastric ulcers. You may also be at risk of developing diabetes, hypertension, chronic fatigue, as well as experiencing impairment in liver and digestive function. On an emotional level, there will be imbalances encompassing concerns about one's physical appearance, apprehension regarding criticism and rejection, as well as broader challenges associated with personal power dynamics.

Upon successfully reestablishing the alignment of this particular chakra, you will experience an elevated sense of self-compassion, coupled with an enhanced level of self-reverence, thereby bestowing upon yourself a newfound state of self-assurance, assertiveness, and autonomy in directing the course of your own life. The fundamental insight to acknowledge is the importance of self-acceptance in all circumstances, as it is solely through this realization that one can actively pursue constructive transformations.

The Green Chakra, situated within the center of the thoracic region, governs and harmonizes the physiological organs and anatomical components situated within its vicinity. Dysfunctions related to this chakra encompass discomfort in the wrists and arms, complications in the shoulders and back, ailments affecting the breasts, as well as illnesses centered in the respiratory and cardiovascular systems, potentially manifesting as asthma. Disparity in emotional states encompasses feelings of solitude-induced anxiety, overarching resentment, ire, envy, and an excessively dependent approach to romantic relationships.

When this chakra is in a state of equilibrium, it facilitates the experience of being reliable and relied upon, magnanimous, empathetic, affectionate, appreciative, and elated. This energy system provides us with an insight into the concept of love.

The Throat Chakra, also known as the Blue Chakra, is located in the region of your neck and its disharmony can manifest as various facial dysfunctions, including complications with the tongue, lips, cheeks, and chin. Additionally, it is possible to observe symptoms such as sore throats, ear infections, ulcers, and potential thyroid complications. Furthermore, it is possible for individuals to experience discomfort in the shoulder and neck regions in this location. In the event of an imbalance in this particular chakra, individuals may encounter emotional challenges such as diminished determination or self-restraint, apprehension regarding the absence of authority in their lives, as well as difficulties in effectively expressing themselves verbally or in writing.

When your throat chakra achieves equilibrium, an unrestricted flow of verbal communication ensues, allowing for effortless dialogue and seamless expression. You demonstrate a remarkable facility in expressing your genuine emotions and effortlessly engaging in attentive listening. This instructional session aims to encourage individuals to express their authentic thoughts and beliefs, despite the inherent challenges that may arise.

The Indigo Chakra, also known as the Brow Chakra, is situated precisely at the center of one's forehead, positioned between the eyebrows. The dissonance resulting from the misalignment of this particular chakra gives rise to challenges concerning the equipoise of your hormones, auditory impairment, epileptic episodes, ocular strain, sinus afflictions, and visual impairment. Additionally, one may observe the presence of headaches, emotional disturbances, difficulties in accurately perceiving oneself, and overall emotional instability. One may encounter difficulties when confronting fears or assimilating knowledge from others, as they may become engrossed in daydreams and possess an excessively active imagination.

When the third eye chakra is harmonized, individuals will experience a heightened sense of concentration, mental clarity, and the ability to differentiate between falsehoods and reality. You possess a heightened level of perceptiveness, enabling you to adeptly discern insights and obtain general wisdom, both from within yourself and from others. This particular chakra provides you with a valuable lesson in perceiving the entirety of a situation, as opposed to merely its individual components.

The Crown Chakra: Situated precisely at the apex of the skull. The presence of disparities in this context gives rise to heightened sensitivity to one's surroundings, encompassing auditory and visual stimuli. One might also observe that the process of acquiring knowledge is subject to heightened complexity, and one might encounter challenges in apprehending the magnitude of this vast universe and comprehending the depths of self-awareness. One may observe a tendency to experience apprehension towards seclusion, frequently engage in excessive rumination, and become confined within inflexible patterns of thinking.

An equilibrium within your crown chakra enables you to exist in the present moment without any perturbations. You have faith in your personal framework of guidance and feel connected to your spiritual essence. The crown chakra imparts the wisdom of being fully present in one's existence and cultivating a state of conscious awareness throughout life.

Upon perusing these depictions, it is conceivable that you may have discerned the presence of certain chakras that are obstructed or experiencing disharmony. The occurrence at hand involves the blocking of one chakra, which subsequently triggers an intensified state of functioning in the remaining chakras as an effort to restore equilibrium. To rectify this issue, it is advisable to commence the spiritual healing process by focusing on the foundational chakra and progressively ascend, meticulously opening and restoring the subsequent energy centers. In the subsequent section, a comprehensive explanation shall be provided on the methodology employed to accomplish this.

WHAT IS CHAKRA

Chakras, which derive from the Sanskrit term meaning circular or spinning discs, serve as the pivotal centers of energy within the human body. These energy vortices are precisely aligned along the central axis of the body. The Chakras are positioned in a sequence along the spinal column, extending from the lowermost point to the highest point at the top of the head.

There exist seven Chakras that possess clusters of nerves, with each primary Chakra serving as an autonomous center of intelligence. This elucidates the fact that Chakras extend beyond mere physical health, encompassing domains tied to faith, emotional well-being, and cognitive functioning.

Prana, an imperceptible force, is a crucial life energy that sustains our vitality, well-being, and vigor. The Nadi, being a conduit for the flow of energy, can give rise to restlessness when there is an obstruction in its path.

In the realm of the energetic body, one finds a multitude of chakras. Engaging in postures such as back bending can effectively foster a harmonious circulation of the heart Chakra, simultaneously revitalizing the individual's immune system, lungs, and heart. This practice serves to facilitate a more compassionate and affectionate way of living. The proper functioning of Chakra involves the harmonization of physical health, mental and emotional well-being, as well as the spiritual aspect of the body, achieved through the absorption and distribution of energy.

Chakra mappings and systems are embodied within a plethora of diverse customs, cultures, religions, and spiritual traditions, encompassing Native and Central American Shamanic traditions, Tibetan Buddhism, Hindu/Indian Yoga systems, and more. Certain theologians believe that there exist implicit allusions to them within the writings of certain mystics.

Chakras in numerous cultural and spiritual traditions bear connections to specific elements, incantations, and hues, thus giving rise to disparities across various regions and belief systems. They serve the dual purpose of facilitating spiritual enlightenment and promoting physical and emotional well-being through energy healing. Chakras, in a state of openness, are regarded as functioning consistently, exhibiting different degrees of activation.

IMPORTANCE OF CHAKRA SYSTEM

In the event that an individual encounters a state of destabalization or physical discomfort, it becomes vital to engage in the activation, clearing, and balancing of one's Chakra system as it plays a significant role in addressing these concerns. This diagnostic tool is highly remarkable, as it effectively discerns blockages, imbalances, and disharmony within the Chakra systems. It is of utmost importance to be cognizant of the choices or habits that have led to or played a role in the discomfort or imbalance, and to consistently and persistently engage in practices aimed at realigning these Chakras so as to foster harmony and promote a thriving existence.

The harmony of the body's various Chakras is interdependent, meaning that an inactive or obstructed Chakra can have a profound impact on the functioning of the others, causing them to become deficient. Consequently, the imbalances created by a blocked Chakra prompt the remaining Chakras to overcompensate in their activity.

REASONS CHAKRAS ARE COLORED

Each chakra exhibits distinct hues or variations in color, albeit with one predominant color prevailing. The colors serve to depict the fundamental purpose of the Chakra. Each color has been assigned a specific role in the rejuvenation of the body. Below are the six atomic radiations, encompassing violet, blue, green, yellow, orange, and dark red, with the seventh, or rose-red, atom dispersing downward through the vortex's central channel.

Chakras are imbued with distinct hues to differentiate one from another; they additionally function as corporeal manifestations to decipher luminous energy through the corporeal senses, thus enabling the exploration of the expansive boundaries of color energy.

Equilibrium, Disequilibrium, And Obstructed Chakras

Similar to the human body, the energy centers are equally susceptible to their environment. This is alternatively referred to as experiencing a blockage or an imbalance. When the pathways are obstructed, energy circulation is impeded; in case of imbalance, there may exist an excess or deficiency of energy within them. Within this chapter, we shall expound upon the manifestations exhibited by chakras that are in a state of equilibrium, discordance, or obstruction.

The Root Chakra

An individual who possesses a well-functioning or harmonious Root Chakra experiences a sense of security and safety. There is a sense of assurance in making decisions to progress, as the foundation beneath our feet is sturdy. Frequent occurrences indicate that the Root Chakra often becomes imbalanced as a result of abrupt and distressing life events, including instances of abandonment or the unfortunate loss of a cherished individual.

Physical Manifestations of an Imbalanced Root Chakra:

Difficulties pertaining to the lower extremities including the legs, hips, feet, knees, and ankles.

Eating disorders

Diarrhea

Constipation

Water retention

Lower back pain

Sciatica

Varicose veins

Psychological Manifestations Associated with an Impeded Root Chakra Flow:

Insecurities often result in an inclination towards a state of constant survival.

Feeling abandoned

Feeling undeserving

Loss of control

Incapable of rendering significant judgments.

Various fears and phobias

Feelings of loneliness

In the event of a blockage in your Root Chakra, you may experience emotions such as melancholy, apprehension, self-doubt, anxieties, and hesitancy. It appears as though there is an absence of emotional catharsis, resulting in an overwhelming perception dominated by a constant state of apprehension. Furthermore, there may be occurrences wherein the Root Chakra exhibits an excessive level of activity. In the eventuality of such an occurrence, the signs of the imbalances will be magnified in their entirety. As an illustration, one potential outcome is that your fear would escalate into a state of irrational paranoia.

The Sacral Chakra

A harmoniously aligned Sacral Chakra will serve as a catalyst for enhanced levels of creativity. Furthermore, one will observe that the experience of pleasure, particularly in its intimate manifestation, is readily attainable. In terms of emotional well-being, you are satisfactory as you currently experience happiness. However, it is important to note that upon encountering certain events, appropriate emotions may gradually emerge. Regardless of the nature of these emotions, you do not experience a sense of vulnerability. To put it differently, there exists an equilibrium in your feelings and emotions. The cultivation of a balanced second chakra will result in the nurturing of symbiotic relations with the external environment, fostering a state of harmonious coexistence. You derive gratification, therefore it is only natural for you to desire others to derive it as well.

Manifestations of Dysfunctional Sacral Chakra:

A diminished sexual drive or experiencing an inability to derive enjoyment from engaging in sexual activities.

Eating disorder

Inability to conceive

Miscarriages

Weight gain

Problems in menstrual cycle

Kidney problems

Sexual disorders

"Psychological Manifestations Associated with an Inharmonious Sacral Chakra:

Lack of joy

Creative blocks

Mood swings

Displaying excessive dependence on others or engaging in numerous casual sexual relationships.

Lack of interest or indifference

Sexual obsessions

Emotions of inadequacy Sense of personal insufficiency

Must consistently strive to satisfy others

Individuals who possess an obstructed Sacral Chakra are frequently those who have experienced childhood neglect or abuse. These individuals frequently perceive themselves as lacking merit or unworthiness of genuine affection. As a result, they exhibit excessive dependency and consistently demonstrate a fervent desire to satisfy others. Because of the absence of a strong emotional connection, they encounter difficulty in maintaining a relationship. The absence of emotional engagement and a lack of demonstrative feelings can be correlated with an obstructed Sacral Chakra.

The Solar Plexus Chakra

The manifestation of a strong third chakra is evidenced through a sense of ambitiousness and an unwavering determination to make progress. There exists a natural inclination towards assuming leadership roles in a manner that facilitates the attainment of harmony. Additionally, you place considerable reliance on your intuition as it frequently guides you towards making accurate judgments.

Manifestations of an Aura Dysfunction in the Solar Plexus Chakra:

Experiencing difficulties in maintaining focus or retaining critical information.

Intestinal disorders

Digestive problems

Metabolic dilemmas

Diabetes

Dermatological conditions such as eczema and acne (attributable to heightened stress levels)

Obesity

Ulcer

Chronic fatigue

"Psychological Manifestations of Dysfunctional Solar Plexus Chakra:

Insufficient regard for oneself and/or others.

Reluctance to be in the limelight

Insufficient self-regard and inadequate self-assurance

In certain scenarios when an excess of energy is present, you may additionally encounter the following:

Excessive self-importance or an inflated sense of self

Extreme introversion or extroversion

Exhibiting a tendency towards assertiveness, or an elevated desire to establish and maintain authority over those in one's vicinity.

Manipulative

Maleficence or encroachment of power

On the contrary, an obstructed solar plexus chakra engenders sensations of immobilization, producing a profound sense of powerlessness and lack of influence. Although you may possess a host of thoughts, it is apparent that you are plagued by confusion and a lack of decisive action. Your level of self-assurance has reached its lowest point yet.

The Heart Chakra

A well-balanced Heart Chakra fosters an interconnectedness not just with one's own physical, mental, and emotional aspects, but also with the external environment. You possess a profound sense of serenity, elation, and conviction, and your decision-making process is characterized by an equitable consideration of both worldly and metaphysical aspects. Your history is widely acknowledged and you possess the capacity to exonerate those who have transgressed against you.

Indications of an Unbalanced Heart Chakra from a Physical Perspective:

Respiratory ailments such as pneumonia and asthma (or other pulmonary conditions)

Breast problems

Discomfort experienced in the region of the upper back and shoulders

Tachycardia and chest pain

Vertigo

Heart diseases

Carpal tunnel syndrome or any other upper extremity disorders

Psychological Manifestations of an Unbalanced Heart Chakra:

Showing a disregard for the feelings or well-being of others

Being unable to forgive

The incapacity to determine whether to heed the rational or emotional inclination

Absence of tranquility (resulting in heightened levels of tension)

Unhappiness

Possessiveness

Inability to trust others

Demonstrating ingratitude; failure to acknowledge and appreciate the bestowed blessings.

Being aloof and cold

An obstructed heart chakra can have adverse effects on individuals. Envision oneself adopting emotional reticence, resulting in a disposition marked by resentment, discontentment, and an inability to openly convey affection towards others. Regrettably, individuals who have an obstructed heart chakra are unable to avail themselves of love, even when it is extended to them. There is a lack of tranquility, as you are disengaged not only from your surroundings, but also from your own being. Your uncertainty stems from your lack of awareness regarding the role you are meant to fulfill.

The Throat Chakra

Possessing the capability to effectively communicate across various dimensions (physical, verbal, and emotional) is a significant attribute associated with the cultivation and sustenance of a harmonious and robust Throat Chakra. An additional skill involves demonstrating effective listening when engaged in communication with others. You possess adept adaptation skills and demonstrate no reservation in your nonverbal communication.

Manifestations of an Unbalanced Throat Chakra:

Constant lying

The tendency to restrain oneself from expressing words or sobs.

Stuttering

The consistent occurrence of a sensation resembling a lump in the throat."

Thyroid conditions such as hyperthyroidism or hypothyroidism

Tonsillitis

Neck and shoulder pain

Engaging in excessive verbal communication or indulging in idle chatter (in relation to an overactive Throat Chakra)

Voice problems

Being tone deaf

Psychological Manifestations of Throat Chakra Imbalance:

Apprehension towards expressing oneself, particularly in a public setting, due to the concern that one's voice will go unheard or the significance of one's words will be overlooked.

Hesitance with words

Lack of receptiveness to others' perspectives.

Shyness

Lack of effective self-expression Difficulty in articulating one's thoughts and feelings Incapacity to communicate effectively

Promise-breaking

Inability to keep secrets

An obstructed Throat Chakra exacerbates the manifestations of the disrupted energy center. For example, one may experience a sense of frustration when faced with the desire to express oneself but concurrently lacking the ability to overcome said frustration. You exhibit a tendency to be reserved, reticent, and encounter difficulties in managing situations.

The Third Eye Chakra

As this pertains to our chakra associated with receptiveness, a well-balanced Third Eye Chakra guarantees the capacity to make sound judgments that encompass both rationality and intuitive discernment. Individuals who possess a strong and balanced Third Eye Chakra have the capacity to cultivate or amplify their extrasensory faculties and establish a profound bond with the cosmic realm. Your perceptions will be robust, and as you embark on a particular voyage, you will experience a sense of being directed.

Manifestations of an Unbalanced Third Eye Chakra on the Physical Level:

Eye problems

Sleep disorders like insomnia

Headaches

Having hallucinations

Hair issues

Psychological Symptoms of Imbalanced Third Eye Chakra:

The circumstances appear to be obscure, particularly in challenging scenarios.

Lack of vision development; at times, the vision may be present but remains unrecognized.

Close mindedness

Irrational anxiety - an individual with an unbalanced Third Eye Chakra experiences apprehension towards both the current and upcoming circumstances, achievements and disappointments, and existence and mortality.

Lack of temporal awareness - frequently inquiring about the current date

Pessimism

An obstructed Third Eye exacerbates the symptoms of imbalance.

The Crown Chakra

Ultimately, we have arrived at the pinnacle of the energy hub. An optimally functioning Crown Chakra will enable you to transcend. Individuals who possess a harmonious state of their primary chakra derive pleasure from life while simultaneously harboring no apprehensions towards mortality, owing to their complete detachment from the material realm. They experience a profound sense of wholeness, as they embody a state of unity in their essence; the concept of accepting oneself will always remain unfaltering, fostering a lasting serenity.

"Manifestations of an Unbalanced Sahasrara Chakra:

Nervous system problems

Neurological disorders

Headaches

Unreasonable sensitivity to light

Autoimmune diseases

Psychiatric conditions such as schizophrenia

Psychological Manifestations of an Imbalanced Sahasrara Energy Center:

Confusion

Helplessness

Sudden disorientation

Alienation extends beyond the realm of the material world, penetrating deeply into the domain of the ethereal.

Occasionally, individuals may experience the sensation of solely inhabiting their thoughts.

Loss of faith

Encountering a plethora of apprehensions.

Feeling apathetic or indifferent

A hindered Crown Chakra can have detrimental effects, to put it mildly. It can be likened to a cascading chain reaction. Illustratively speaking, should one encounter an intensified state of helplessness, a concomitant sentiment of frustration is anticipated to ensue. This frustration will not only result in an increased sense of powerlessness, but also give rise to feelings of fear and depression.

Now that this has been clarified, we will now progress to the subsequent section which deals with the subject of Chakra Healing.

The Seven Chakras

Chakras consist of a framework of seven fundamental elements, commonly known as "the 7 Chakras System." Nevertheless, there is more to consider. Indeed, a total of 114 Chakras have been delineated, and it is worth considering that Chakras permeate throughout our entire physiology, as we often tend to exclusively focus on the energy within our bodies, neglecting to acknowledge the presence of these energy centers in our other bodily constituents. To provide absolute clarity, it is imperative to acknowledge that the 7 Chakras serve as the central pillars that facilitate alignment and bolster all other components within the human physique.

Therefore, irrespective of the number of Chakras that may exist, it is advisable to maintain a connection solely with these 7 Chakras as they will facilitate the harmonization of your physical and spiritual being. The energy of chakras is evident in various locations within the body and is characterized by distinct colors, corresponding specifically to different parts of the human anatomy, particularly the spinal cord. Specifically, when we strive to enhance the functionality of those central energies according to our desired objectives, it is referred to as the equilibrium or recuperation of the Chakras. On the other hand, should these energies traverse a downward-to-upward trajectory, it is probable that spiritual healing will ensue and commence its efficacy, resulting in physical and mental well-being.

Earlier, we made reference to the rainbow river; hence, we are curious about its appearance. The seven Chakras are characterized by distinct colors and positioned in various locations, maintaining a synchronized alignment. Their hues resemble the full spectrum of the prismatic rainbow. This range of hues, as is commonly understood, serves as the fundamental basis for all perceivable colors. Furthermore, it should be noted that the concept of color entails a distinctive vibrational quality associated with each individual hue. The identical principle is likewise applicable to the circulation of energy in the Chakras' circular structure across their respective chromatic components. For instance, red possesses the lengthiest and most leisurely wavelength and vibration, thereby enabling us to discern this hue for its inherent warmth. Additionally, the color violet also pertains to this topic. It possesses the most abbreviated and rapid wavelength and vibration, resulting in our perception of it as a predominantly chilly and ordinary hue.

Within the spectral range between the hues of red and violet, the five remaining colors elegantly oscillate in a sequential arrangement dictated by variations in wavelength and velocity. This fundamental knowledge holds significant importance, as even contemporary science has demonstrated that specific colors possess the ability to stimulate mental activity and influence instinctual behavior. Undoubtedly, we each possess a preferred hue that illuminates our day. Therefore, we return to the seven hues that remain constrained within the corporeal vessel of the human being. Every one of them is linked to an organ or gland that presides over a distinct region of the body. This is precisely why Chakras have been discovered and extensively investigated, in order to unveil the means of exerting spiritual control. The sequencing of the Chakras follows a ascending pattern, ascending from the base of the body towards the crown at its pinnacle. The journey commences with the color red, symbolizing the fundamental essence, and progresses through the variegated vibrational spectrum of each Chakra, culminating in the profound hue of violet, representing the spiritual pinnacle.

The Root Chakra

Envision a scenario where a tree exists devoid of any discernible root structure. It would not even assume the form of a tree. The intricate complexities of human existence can be likened to that of a tree, thus giving rise to the term "life tree." The root Chakra embodies emotional energies pertaining to stability in one's existence, fostering a profound and unyielding sense of connection to ancestral origins, thereby facilitating the sustenance required for the growth and vitality of one's life's endeavors. It is situated in the lower region of the body, adjacent to the pelvic region and in proximity to the adrenal gland. It is likewise referred to as the endurance of Chakra, comparable to the manner in which we establish and endure within our existence. Therefore, if you encounter challenges establishing stability in your life, it is possible that you are experiencing an imbalance in your Root Chakra.

The general consensus is that it is perceived as the most challenging one to handle. Presently, the prevailing sentiment of insecurity within society is widely observed, thereby establishing a clear correlation. Due to the nature of the root Chakra, it primarily focuses on fostering a sense of grounding and stability. If you experience a tendency to perceive oneself as lacking stability or being disconnected, it becomes imperative to address the very foundation of one's existence, the core of our establishment, and the emotions that arise from it. Experiencing feelings of vulnerability, insecurity, and a lack of security can indicate an imbalance in the root Chakra. To be more exact, the blocking of this energy can give rise to a range of challenges, including financial instability, disruptions in personal well-being, increased anxiety, and a sense of disorientation regarding one's sense of belonging. On the other hand, when the root Chakra is in a state of optimal health, commonly referred to as "equilibrium," a range of positive indications often emerge such as a sense of inner peace, assurance, and imperviousness to potential vulnerabilities. Regardless of your location, you experience a steadfast sense of grounding within your personal boundaries. Fundamentally, you experience a profound sense of joy in simply existing.

Excessive indications of the Root Chakra can manifest as an augmented inclination towards materialism or avarice. It implies a proclivity towards coveting wealth and influence. Researchers associate the fundamental Chakra, namely the root Chakra, with the anatomical entity known as the Cauda Equina, denoting the collective assemblage of spinal nerves and spinal nerve roots. It appears to resemble the intricate network of roots found in a tree, which serves to supply nerves to the human body's lower extremities, including the feet, ankles, legs, and hips, enabling a direct connection to the foundation. Such mundane sensory experiences are essential for maintaining equilibrium and executing each stride with serenity in corporeal existence, thereby attaining a state of satisfaction facilitated by a well-functioning Cauda Equina. When one possesses the ability to move unrestricted, attain financial autonomy, enjoy unrestricted mobility, experience acceptance and hospitality wherever they journey, and find contentment in their surroundings. Indeed, it is apparent that achieving this outcome is our desired objective in life. Nobody desires to experience feelings of distrust, exclusion, or isolation amidst a populace.

Nevertheless, it is contingent upon your personal discretion. The efficacy with which you regulate and maintain equilibrium within your root chakras significantly influences your ability to establish stability in your life. Should you neglect to maintain proper balance in your Root Chakra, you may encounter difficulties in progressing, experience discontentment in various aspects of your life, struggle to locate a sense of belonging, and encounter challenges when attempting to assimilate into different environments. Perhaps this concept is now more recognizable, as it commonly occurs among the majority of individuals.

Overview of the Foundational Chakra

Position: The root Chakra can be found situated at the lowermost point of the spinal column, specifically encompassing the initial three vertebrae of the pelvic region within the human anatomy. We deemed it a fundamental element that remains in the lower level, yet highly crucial in establishing the foundation for us.

Color attribute: It is connected to the hue red, which embodies the most measured vibration in terms of wavelength among colors.

Sangkrit: It is known as Muladhara in the context of Sangkrit.

Grounding & Accountability: The fundamental basis for this Chakra entails a fundamental sense of reliance, stemming from the fact that individuals feel most connected to the Earth when they assume a seated or reclined position. It corresponds to the sensation of rootedness or stability, possessing economic autonomy, assurance, and well-being irrespective of location, architectural integrity and optimal composition, and fundamental existential sustenance. Evidently, it serves as the foundational essence upon which the life cycle of individuals relies. In the same way that individuals strive for a life devoid of instability, the acquisition of skills to harmonize the root Chakra proves to be highly beneficial.

Yoga Asana and Chant: There exists a specific yogic posture that can be diligently engaged in to foster the activation of the Root Chakra, which has been observed to be in a state of unresponsiveness. This particular pose is known as the tree pose. It bears resemblance to how we previously elucidated your foundational Chakra as the fundamental nexus of your life essence. In conjunction with this posture, we introduce the hand mudra for this particular Chakra. You can achieve this by bringing your index finger into contact with your thumb, and subsequently extending your arms so that both hands rest upon the knees, with the arms fully extended.

Indicators of a harmonized or activated Root Chakra can be observed through one's level of grounding, unwavering composure, fearlessness, and consequent feelings of serenity. Indications of an excessive level of activity in this regard are a heightened sense of materialism and a strong desire for power. In the interim, indications of an obstructed or unbalanced Root Chakra manifest as persistent apprehension towards instability or feeling lost, coupled with bouts of anxiety.

There exist various activities that you can engage in to restore equilibrium to your root Chakra. Engaging in greater frequency of grounding, such as regularly allowing your bare feet to make direct contact with the earth's surface, enables a heightened sense of connection with the natural world. Another additional activity to consider is engaging in regular leisurely strolls outdoors, preferably in a setting that you find amenable. Immerse yourself in the tranquility of a garden, enveloped by the natural world, to foster a heightened sense of harmony with nature. Cultivating and fostering plants can aid in the establishment of equilibrium and robustness in your root Chakra.

Furthermore, by associating this Chakra with its corresponding hue, one can also facilitate a harmonious connection with the root Chakra. You can achieve this by adorning yourself in garments of crimson hue, directing your gaze towards objects of the same scarlet shade, and immersing yourself in the sensory experience it elicits. One can enhance and harmonize their root energy by consuming nourishing foods of a red hue, such as red curry, raspberries, strawberries, pomegranate seeds, and a crimson apple. There are individuals who engage in Chakras meditation utilizing stones, crystals, and the aromatic qualities of essential oils. According to the recommendation of a recognized authority in the field of yoga, Robin Krasny, she indicated that employing essential oils such as patchouli, frankincense, and cedarwood, as well as incorporating the use of crystals or gemstones like garnet, ruby, or red stone, can effectively stimulate and harmonize the root Chakra, leading to its complete activation and alignment with one's life force.

The Sacral Chakra

The Sacral Chakra is situated in close proximity to the Root Chakra, in the lower region. To be more exact, the current Chakra operates in a distinct manner when compared to its predecessor, primarily serving as a conduit for the linkage between internal energy and external forces. The Sacral Chakra pertains to the integration of emotional energies and one's ability to establish meaningful connections with oneself and others. Furthermore, it is referred to as the 'Sacral Chakra' due to its regulation and receptivity to intense emotions and expressions of sexuality. Based on the location within the lower abdominal region, it resides at the intermediary point between the connection and the association. Specifically, the challenges encountered in maintaining a long-term relationship or the difficulties experienced in navigating relationships may stem from an imbalance within the Sacral Chakra.

Regarding the matter of procreation, it is the sacral nerves that furnish the vital energy to the reproductive organs. The process of reproduction serves as a means of physical connection and sustenance of the bond between partners. As a result, it is evident that individuals of both genders are likely to be cognizant of this vital force originating from the Sacral Chakra.

Hence, for the sake of precision, it can be stated that this Chakra embodies the energetic interplay between societal dynamics and human sexuality. Individuals may experience intense emotions, and the sensation of fervor is inherently influenced by their personal preferences as well. Nevertheless, in the event of one possessing excessive physical appeal or alternatively, being situated at the lower end of the attractiveness spectrum, the consequence will invariably manifest as an inherent disruption to the equilibrium of the Sacral Chakra. Hence, achieving equilibrium in this Chakra necessitates the experience of delight, sensuousness, gratification, nurturance, and profound sentiments such as fervor and sanguinity.

The obstructed or disrupted sacral Chakra can manifest as a diminished sexual drive or an unhealthy state of your intimate relationships, possibly stemming from a limited sense of social engagement or a sense of disengagement from society. It discerns our gender, reproductive system, and aspects such as gratification, aversion to close connections resulting in complete absence of intimacy, absence of originality or its deficiency, as well as experiencing profound solitude or seclusion. It exerts a detrimental impact on the functioning of the Sacral Chakra.

However, conversely, an excessively stimulated sacral Chakra can prove to be troubling as it leads to excessive rumination or heightened emotional states, potentially causing one to exhibit hedonistic tendencies, engage in compulsive sexual behaviors, or display manipulative tendencies. Hence, it is imperative for us to maintain a heightened sense of awareness in order to avoid succumbing to the overwhelming influence of our emotions and sexuality. One might encounter difficulty assimilating into various social groups, or alternatively, one may experience profound feelings of solitude when in isolation.

Nevertheless, attaining equilibrium within the Sacral Chakra can prove to be highly beneficial for individuals within the reproductive stages of their lives. It will enhance your fertility and alleviate the challenges associated with pregnancy and childbirth. Furthermore, the vitality emanating from the Sacral Chakra actively promotes interpersonal bonds, fostering a sense of connectedness with individuals in one's social sphere, including friends and family. We can include parents, teachers, and even individuals who are not known to the child. The manner in which you assimilate yourself into social circles may be influenced by the vibrational energy of this particular Chakra. When experiencing a sense of optimism and self-assurance, individuals tend to exhibit increased levels of both smiling and conversing. These attributes have the potential to enhance your appeal and facilitate engagement with individuals.

Establishing A Connection With Your Chakras And Cultivating Self-Awareness

The chakras are distinct components of their energy system, implying that there is no universally effective method for harmonizing all of them. Each of these practices necessitates exertion on distinct bodily regions, and the primary measure in acquainting oneself with the chakras (even prior to determining their potential imbalance) involves establishing a connection with them.

Several classifications exist for the potential malfunctions that can occur within your chakras. The initial point of consideration is that they are experiencing obstruction or complete obstruction. This occurs as a consequence of a disturbance in the balance of our daily routines. Some commonly experienced sources of anguish include suffering induced by tragic events, the emotional ramifications of loss, and the subsequent bereavement that follows. Significant hindrances within the chakra energetic pathways can also be instigated by more minor factors, including occupational stress, performance-related anxiety, interpersonal connections apprehension, and prevailing fear. A significant number of individuals experience a perpetual state of apprehension, and this is a matter that cannot be fully rectified instantaneously. In order to have any prospect of overcoming it, it is crucial for you to acknowledge the fear that resides within you. The specific chakra that becomes obstructed will vary depending on the nature of the disturbance or emotion you are encountering. To illustrate, the termination of a romantic relationship may lead to an impediment in the heart chakra, with the possibility of concurrent blockages in other interconnected chakras. We shall delve deeper into this matter during the upcoming chapter three).

When certain chakras become excessively obstructed in allowing the flow of energy, they emit a 'distress signal' to ascertain the attention of other chakras. The remaining chakras may respond by becoming unsealed and absorbing a surplus of energy, at times surpassing their capacity to effectively manage it. This can instigate a heightened emotional sensitivity, induce feelings of anxiety, and induce stress— precisely the issues that initially led to the blockages.

When a chakra is blocked it can cause other chakras to become too open, likewise of a chakra is too open and receiving too much energy it can cause other chakras to become blocked—this is all a cyclic process, which is why it is important to determine the root cause of your imbalance and correct it right away.

The chakras exist within us all, yet each individual necessitates personalized approaches to connect with them and deepen self-consciousness. This holds particular significance for individuals who are in the initial stages of embarking on the journey towards attaining chakra health and equilibrium. With that being stated, there exist various approaches—most of which are straightforward! There are several commendable methods available to acquaint oneself with their respective system.

Every individual chakra possesses its distinct manner of communication. This entails that achieving chakra equilibrium necessitates attentive listening to the messages they convey. How can one engage in auditory perception of something that is inaudible? It is imperative that you acquire the skill of auditory perception. This entails the acquisition of skills in establishing a connection with one's physical self and attentively perceiving its communication. Attempting to immediately engage in chakra balancing through practices such as yoga, meditation, and dietary adjustments might prove challenging (although individual experiences may vary). Nonetheless, by dedicating some time to reestablishing a connection with your body, you will discover that attuning to its needs becomes a far more effortless endeavor.

In our everyday lives, we frequently exert extraordinary efforts to accommodate the needs and desires of others, sometimes at the expense of neglecting our own well-being, which is the utmost significance. We frequently relegate our emotions, desires, and needs to a secondary position. Within our societal construct, selflessness is widely regarded as a virtue that holds potential for goodness. Ultimately, to provide assistance and strive for a fulfilling and contented life, it becomes imperative to cultivate a measure of self-centeredness. It is not centered around indulgence; rather, it pertains to the cultivation of self-respect and the preservation of our personal well-being.

To accomplish this task, it is imperative that we allocate the necessary time to acquaint ourselves with both our emotional states and the bodily sensations that occur. Presented below are several strategies aimed at assisting individuals in developing emotional awareness. Please bear in mind that if you disregard them, you inevitably neglect the well-being of your chakras. They are intricately interconnected at the most profound depths, and in order to facilitate the restoration of your chakras, it is imperative that you possess a deep understanding of yourself. The vast majority of individuals lack a meaningful connection with their physical and spiritual selves. Nevertheless, this deficiency can be rectified by according careful consideration to these aspects.

The majority of individuals have experienced significant levels of adversity in their lives and frequently resort to coping mechanisms that are not conducive to their overall well-being. Many individuals have undergone distressing incidents, which, even if they occurred in the past, can continue to influence our chakras at present. It is of utmost importance to acknowledge and allow the emergence of such a form of distress.

The task of acknowledging and authentically experiencing one's emotions can present a challenge, yet it is an unequivital requirement. You may experience a multitude of emotions simultaneously, leading to a sense of being overburdened. Just breath. It won't last forever. Please bear in mind that you are currently on the path to addressing those emotions, restoring balance to your chakras, and ultimately experiencing a more fulfilling existence.

Begin with a small practice. If you have not engaged in meditation previously, there is no need for concern. This does not precisely involve meditation itself, but rather serves as a precursor to the practice or an introductory experience. This process is expeditious, effortless, and (comparatively) devoid of discomfort. The objective of this practice is akin to the initial step in acquainting oneself with the concept of chakra energy and its harmonization. This process is straightforward and does not necessitate a mantra, merely a small allocation of your time. You are at liberty to allocate as much time as desired to this matter, yet it is crucial to note that the greater the duration you dedicate to contemplation, the greater the wealth of insights you shall acquire, leading to an enhanced ability to recuperate.

Withdraw yourself from all forms of commotion and activity. Seek out a secluded and tranquil space, free from any potential disturbances, where you can have utmost privacy. Please refrain from bringing your mobile device into the specified area. Ensure that you are dressed in loose and comfortable attire. Please ensure that you have in your possession a pencil and a sheet of paper for the purpose of writing.

This activity solely entails the exercise of cognitive faculties. While it may not be classified strictly as a meditation, it serves as a valuable initial foray into the practice, which will become essential in the future. With that being stated, it would be advisable for you to assume a supine position on the floor.

Please shut your eyes and direct your attention towards your inner self. Reflect upon your day and the emotions you experienced. It is highly probable that you did not experience a flawless day devoid of any challenges. Even supposing that you did consider the matter, reflect upon the days preceding this. What factors caused you significant distress, which you believed to be outside the realm of your influence? What were the emotions of fear, annoyance, and anguish that you experienced during that time?

This can manifest as work-related stressors, familial or marital issues, or emotional burdens resulting from the failure to attain individual aspirations. These emotions have the potential to endure for an extended period of time, originating from experiences of great sorrow or psychological distress. Alternatively, they may be transient in nature, arising from the challenges and circumstances of daily existence. It is imperative at this moment that you permit yourself to experience these emotions. Acknowledge their presence and be cognizant of their existence. This procedure may span a short duration of time, ranging from a few brief moments to a few extended hours. Please bear in mind that the effort you invest will yield corresponding results, therefore allocate a sufficient amount of time.

Please take a moment to contemplate these emotions. Take pleasure in them and the manner in which they have exerted a detrimental influence on you. Ultimately, transcribe them onto a sheet of paper in the form of a comprehensive enumeration. Please peruse the list privately and commit it to memory. It can encompass items that were previously unfamiliar or beyond your immediate recognition, and this presents a positive outcome. This inventory serves as an instrument for self-recognition, yet it does not encompass your authentic essence. One's authentic nature remains unaffected by such emotions as it possesses the ability to effectively address them.

One illustration of a roster could manifest in the subsequent manner:

• The emotions that have an adverse impact on me:

• Pressure imparted by my employer

• Dissolution of a romantic relationship • Termination of a partnership • Disintegration of a romantic affiliation • Conclusion of an intimate connection

• Concern regarding the payment of my mortgage • Apprehension about meeting my mortgage obligations • Anxiousness regarding the timely settlement of my mortgage • Distress over the financial responsibility to pay my mortgage • Unease over the potential inability to fulfill my mortgage payments

I am concerned about the possibility that my partner may be engaging in infidelity.

- Concerned about my ability to meet my objectives

- Concerns pertaining to friendships or social connections

- Apprehension regarding the lack of acceptance or potential judgment from others.

- Concern about the potential loss of my employment

- Mortal apprehension

- Anguish due to the passing of my beloved relative

Your catalog may comprise four to five times the amount of information stated or half of it. The crucial aspect lies in your ability to acknowledge these adverse emotions and document them. This enables you to gain a preliminary self-awareness prior to embarking on the investigation of potential imbalances in your chakras.

Preparing For Meditation

In order to commence the practice of meditation, one must first acquire the ability to channel their energies effectively. It is imperative that you acquire the ability to free your mind from anger and negative thoughts. In order to facilitate personal healing and cultivate a state of increased spiritual awareness, it is imperative to prioritize the release of detrimental energy within oneself. When one's mind is consumed by anger and negative thoughts, the likelihood of experiencing this enriching blessing becomes significantly diminished. Your thoughts are preoccupied, hindering your ability to perceive it. As such, a certain amount of training is imperative in order to attain that state of comprehension. To attain this elevated state, one must cultivate a disposition of patience and open-mindedness. This task presents a varying degree of difficulty depending on individual aptitude, yet with diligent practice, one can attain enlightenment.

Prior to commencing your meditation practice, it is advisable to locate a space that possesses qualities of serenity, tranquility, and personal significance. Engage in the pursuit of discovering a location that instills within you an immense sense of inspiration. I opt for an elevated location, preferably at the pinnacle of a hill, affording me unobstructed vistas that extend for several miles. Alternatively, I would relish a secluded enclave on a shoreline, enabling me to witness the graceful descent or ascent of the sun. Select a location that holds personal significance and serves as a source of spiritual inspiration for you. Your designated area could be a specific room within the confines of your residence. Wherever it may be located, its presence should impart tranquility and serenity upon you.

You would prefer to avoid a multitude of distractions. Please ensure that you deactivate all alarms, ringers, and notifications. Please relocate all domestic animals from the proximity of your chosen meditation area. You are advised to choose loose and comfortable attire. It is advisable to consume a light meal prior to commencing meditation. You would not wish to experience the disruption caused by the audible rumblings of hunger. If you desire, you may engage in listening to calming meditative melodies. One can discover appropriate music for meditation on YouTube through the process of conducting a search specifically for meditation music. If you lean towards silence, that is also acceptable.

It is advisable to attain a state of mental relaxation prior to commencing the meditation procedure. Find a comfortable seating position on the floor or assume a kneeling posture while resting on a meditation cushion. It is widely recognized that the root chakra plays a crucial role in enabling an individual to experience a sense of stability in their existence. When engaging in meditation, it is imperative to bear in mind that the posture one assumes during this practice can significantly impact the functioning of this particular chakra. As an illustration, let us consider the scenario where one occupies a seating position that permits the tendency for one's back to adopt a slouched posture; as a consequence, the alignment of this specific chakra would be displaced from its harmonious position along the spine. As a result, the posture you assume during meditation holds significant importance. In cases where sitting on the floor is not feasible, one may opt to occupy a rigid chair while ensuring that the spinal column remains aligned in an upright position, without reclining in any way. It is advisable to maintain flat positioning of your feet on the floor in order to establish a sense of grounding. It is important to ensure that one maintains a straight back, with an appropriate degree of flexibility and avoid excessive rigidity. In actuality, any seating arrangement will suffice. Ensure that you are experiencing a sense of comfort and relaxation, while maintaining an upright posture. Assuming a reclined position may be considered as a viable alternative, although it is highly advisable to exercise caution and refrain from inadvertently succumbing to slumber.

After assuming a comfortable posture, proceed to engage in slow and deliberate inhalation and exhalation. It is essential to ensure that you are allocating sufficient time to thoroughly inhale, allowing for the full expansion of your lungs and abdomen. Breathe out with a relaxed rhythm. Focus on your breath. Direct your attention to the sensation of the air entering your lungs and notice the ensuing tranquility when you exhale. Make a concerted effort to maintain mindfulness by directing your attention towards your breath, and in the event that other thoughts arise, promptly acknowledge them before releasing them. Continue practicing this deep breathing technique until you begin to experience a state of full relaxation.

www.ingramcontent.com/pod-product-compliance
Lightning Source LLC
Chambersburg PA
CBHW050234120526
44590CB00016B/2087